PERENNIAL
NOTES FROM A WEATHERPROOF JOURNAL
BEN ARMSTRONG

Published in the United Kingdom in 2019
by The Knives Forks And Spoons Press,
51 Pipit Avenue,
Newton-le-Willows,
Merseyside,
WA12 9RG.

ISBN 978-1-912211-34-0

Copyright © Ben Armstrong, 2019.

The right of Ben Armstrong to be identified as the author of this work has been asserted by them in accordance with the Copyrights, Designs and Patents Act of 1988. All rights reserved. No part of this publication may be reproduced, stored in a retrieval system, transmitted in any form or by any means, electronic, photocopying, recording or otherwise, without prior permission of the publisher.

Acknowledgements:

Versions of 'The Blue Ringed Octopus', '22 Ocean Terminal', 'Cracked Map', 'Homer's Ring', 'Lonely Genus', 'Driftwood I – IV', 'Colossal', 'Cracked Map' 'Berwick's Jaw' and 'Atlas' in *Leaveners*. 'Driftwood I', 'pygmy offering' in *Warwick Dodo*. 'Lonely Genus' was exhibited in the P Café, Stirchley, November 2015. Works on Pages 30-35 named after songs composed by Richard D. James.

CONTENTS

Perennial   9

I-Mollusca   11
    hello.   13
    cracked map   14
    love is a boo m e r a   n g   15
    Nick Cave ruined my life   16
    driftwood I   17
    driftwood II   18
    spond   19
    driftwood III   20
    pickles   21
    driftwood IV   22
    wavy-dash   23
    song   24

II-Wish you were here   25
    memory wanes, &   27
    freezing grief   28
    [spray]   29
    kladfvgbung micshk   30
    Vordhosbn   31
    Mt Saint Michel + St Michael's Mount   32
    Btoum-Roumada   33
    Jynweythek   34
    Beskhu3epnm   35
    by divinity or unfavourable mutation (a murder)   36
    dawn   37
    22 Ocean Terminal   38

III-Ouroboros   39

   [bandstand blues]   41

   Poseidon   42

   pygmy offering   43

   homer's ring   44

   a breath   45

   atlas   46

   The Blue Ringed Octopus   47

   old bar   48

   Coca Cola Focus Group   49

   endless   50

   lonely genus   51

   Berwick's Jaw   52

   colossal   53

   soulcollector I   54

   ?   55

   ?...   56

   the pier   57

Special acknowledgements to Robert Francis and all at Permission to Speak for allowing me the space to perform new works, several of which are found – finished – in this collection. And to Sander Van Der Wel for his photography of Scheveningen: a place so important to these poems, captured impeccably.

David Morley, I am indebted to you for your tutelage and help in shaping both this collection and my wider work. Thanks also to Luke Kennard, whose sharp wit and biting sarcasm influence me such that his poetry would probably be found here, verbatim, if copyright law permitted.

Eternal thanks to all those who have supported me in writing these poems and I apologise profusely if you find unwelcome similarities between the characters in this collection and yourselves. It wasn't always intentional.

"How much time would you even say has passed, so far?"

– David Foster Wallace, *Good Old Neon*

I – Mollusca

I – Mollusca

hello.

the end of coco pops,
the end of us:
                it began in
medias res with a smile.

liquefy now into me
begin that everlasting sleep
which, since god knows when
has been coming to you
                all too soon.

cracked map

already
      we are boldly launched upon the deep

glared at by elliptical crags
plotted onto maps by dolphin   s o n a r)))

Have Travel! bleats the ghost of a
kingfisher felled in a forever war,
its history hidden in a conch.

two bouldered whales play
scylla / charybdis,
skim stones
on the   elastic sea
threatening peace

tandem eyebrows raised at
passing ships, slipped in from
foreign ports

& on these ships — as I am —
turbulence infests our mouths
choking out surf

[toasting to you]   /a *prost!* on dead ears/
I stay below deck
      lighting candles in portholes,
lightning words from a quill.

commuting each night with a wraith,
it occurs to me that we could all be dreaming or
      /ghosts at the feast/
contained within 35mm reels,
drowning in dust.

love is a boo m e r a   n g

put your ear to the conch –
let it remember long lost lovers
torn away by gargantuan tides
the way the mussels are
ripped from the rocks in a
s
  h
    e
     e
       r
drop
from the water table – all is still.
can you hear the conch shell
as it relays and rebounds your
beating   heart
       back at you
as the pulse of a boomerang?

when your dad rang
round and left/ your soul
spun into my palms
and   off
                     into the distance⹁ɔnɐʇsib

the semblance of a ringing tuning fork
is all you have left
now,
an after-touch of breath.

Ben Armstrong

Nick Cave ruined my life

Nick Cave's bad seeds
gestate in my mind – steal my quips
for use by their two-horned suited and booted
Nick Cave. Braces popping, telling me to fuck right off,
threatening me with another covers album – I see him
on an album cover with a piercing gaze levelled just at me,
Lazarus – I did the digging.
The Lyre of Orpheus came to me –
into my arms – after a successful eBay bid.
The Mercy Seat was a pet name for my recently
installed toilet of which I was immensely proud and
Tupelo was the name of my dog Warren Ellis murdered with a
violin he was playing as a guitar back in 1993.

Nick "Cavernous" Cave
bereft of ideas stole mine
and ruined my life
a real Mephistopheles
a bad seed   a wretch.

His platinum records jostle for space on my mantelpiece.

driftwood I

there was a moment
when we were all there in vintage
nineteen seventies
progressive rock t-shirts, Camel
Goblin, ELP
Fragile - Yes, then I saw your face
reflected in an
ophelian stream which, charged with
azure sent it, shot
across the surface of my eyes

& awoke me from a vicious dream in polyrhythmic starts. This is not science-fiction but
I believe it is possible that we can rob banks with semi
automatic weapons, program ourselves to fly over high-rises, defeat squads of robot squid.

this is not science
fiction,
                but there is always death
  in sleep.

driftwood II

a death by water? perhaps the one that
lays and waits in silt, possessing anemones,
tickling your optic nerve until you
just can't take it anymore, submitting to blindness.
                         your body caked in ink, drowned.

later you appear to me
                             mummified in a fry of eels.
I have no idea
       how it came
to be this way.

spond
for c.c.

… and I remember the day I said
I'd make a poet of you. You were
looking at the stars and grasping for
symbols on the cusp of the shores;
the car window the stand-in for that larger barrier
screening you off from the world's hurly burly.

I was always a sceptic but the lines
on your palms were my constellations.

wednesday, when I mentioned
in what you assumed was
passing that the tides were
higher now than this time
last year –
your nebulous eyes, burnt out,
fidgeted in their sockets,
            sad friends.

that day,
was it you or I who was the pupil?

driftwood III

the   bream   oscillate
                          across   my   REM   eyes,
                                  seaweed brushing against me
  as a passing commuter tends to
        with purely transcribed, false affection.

w h a t is my n a m e?[1] // w h ere a m I[2] // w hati sthis[3]

I realise I have never known the phenomenon of "surprise."

a pacemaker is passed on to me
– a gift from the lungs of
low-lying rock –
                & keeps me
steadily
precisely
      alive.

pickles

the sun blurts out rays;
you are upon me before I know it.

vibrating ring alerts me to your presence
at the bar where there's all the saucy goings on.

bottled up explosion bolts me
from my perch; you look so ripe.

gherkin-jabbed, sea-salted – but
tempered with reams of dough.

calloused bun molests my senses,
my whole posture mirrored in your eyes,

a mugshot of a desperate man.
pickle me with your makeshift lunchbox/

        your large chopping board/
                /your frilly paper garnish.
caress me
as the sea

comes in.

I hope you find me as irresistible as
I find you.

driftwood IV

larks tongues   rescue me
aspect ratios   confuse me
portmanteau   exaggerates me
driftwood   levies me

you/lost/mouth/sparks/
your/clarity///horatian////whole/
you/invigorate////shortpoems///
with/your/wormed/prose/

~ ~ ~ ~ ~ ~ your sated
   sigh moves through me
these saline   songs we sang of the sea
 carry   me
to
agartha

wavy-dash

Wounded raves in the air, collapse into dust –
It had been a long wet spring, watching the sea rust, (3)
reading *'doubts concerning mirror neurons'*, (8)
folding origami (4)
– flying in haiku across room-sized spaces. (9)
Dusk out of oxygen, staving away the blues
of disintegrating blind winter.
                                      It won't be long.

song

the aegean
sea glows red and
the coast lit up
like sanskrit dead
but boiling up
off of the page
as broiled ink
and

sink sailor sink
blink and you'll –

see, you'll miss it.

II – Wish you were here

II – Wish you were here

memory wanes, &

I'm eating brains out of crisp packets
reversing them to fashion
mirrored skin-suits.
      [& in these mirrors]
     smokey
    bacon
   hands
dig into corners, fascinating themselves
as coroners
do with still cold corpses //
as gardeners do
with ready salted earth.
    r e b i r t h – we expect it to be glamourous
          [why] ?
there are no phoenix flames to nurse us
   no eruption of hope/
      rapture
      [no] !
It's always some
     slow
[excruciating] thing, delivered by
razed fingers and foreign thumbs.

a five day plan to change your life –
by   ???
I know that na ….   [memory wanes]

on day one, we are told to fold crisp packets
into kites
//
& by day five, the moon's light has swallowed me
whole o

Ben Armstrong

freezing grief

I first lay eyes on you in Reykjavik,
a whorl of breath and blood

bark fractured with a truncheon or night-stick.
you still smell of kindling

it's night when I watch your roots flicker out
        with the lights
a slip on the ice smashed you into silence

and though I cannot speak a word of Icelandic,
I am an instrumental tourist,
wordlessly majestic.

listen closely to the reverb decayinginginging ng
to see which of us falls
                the
  furthest.

organ blasts from the churches)))

tell me – which icicle shines the sharpest
when the last of the sun fades into the forests.

gorgon snakes from your lips = = =

you answer in tongues, or is it Icelandic-
you, I, the wind a triptych,
calcifying bones.

[spray]

I decided
that I loved you
                    a while after we finished looking at the
Great Wave.
~

I'm a chip off the old woodblock
always moving
I   n   c   r   e   m entally
closer
to killing you
~

Pequodian sea -
lost   in you
and you in me.
two: okinami.
~

I declared a lot right there and then.
later, heart harpooned.
Smithereen, I told you —
"never iceberg me again".

Ben Armstrong

kladfvgbung micshk

micshklanious michael
stockpiles change in his sofa
by day, is a prostitute
by night.
he has thousands of items
of clothing
stored in rusty pipes – he's as
      passive as a sundial,
           as lethal as a bath.

pedantic m.m. tars and
feathers his whole garden
by day,
a ruse to commit bad things
upon worms when the sun sets
and sundials fall asleep, when
birdbaths are home to algae
he strikes –
fierce as genetics,
timely as a birth.

Vordhosbn

travelling on a one
way to Vordhosbn: the
air hangs itself out to dry
on long-since frosted glass.
the washing line expends itself half way
out into the wasteland, the glimmer
the rainbow left behind has vanished. the
order of nature clicks into place sometime
after we pass Btoum. in my brain synapses spring
into life as the mountain points to a smaller brother
out of the window, divisible by the tracks.

I see an effigy of burning knapsacks as we leave Kesson.

Ben Armstrong

Mt Saint Michel + St Michael's Mount

Mount:
We're out on the high seas.
Slung around we're matchstick men,
every breath is fought for as the next catch.
The oyster engulfs the pearl.

Michael:
The fierce genitalia of the sea, the horror stories
tentacled round us at parties by the fire.
The time we all almost drowned.
Flames flecked our innocence, then.

Michel:
The trident forced down our throats.
By the throat, the pristine maw.
We didn't know we'd grown limbs, yet.
The sky turns azure in the moment where –

?:
The pigment of the ocean, congeals,
reveals a fresh breath.

Btoum-Roumada

at
my
wedding,
I see roumada
flowing, a huge
mechanical flower,
lauding over the buffet table.

I realise I have made an error of
disastrous proportions sometime
after the vows, maybe two years,
forty.

hindsight - that grandfather clock in my living room
                                        — t i c k s   o n .

Ben Armstrong

Jynweythek

and it all started per se
when the pianos parsed their
keys and played themselves.

I became the elephant
in the room then, the flat footed lock jawed
lurcher. The years of intonation
carefully sparse smashed
upon my head
in a
    piano
    piano
     piano
    piano

  dr   op

i'm grey
between black
and _____ keys.

Beskhu3epnm

the way the pins move
the way
this makes me feel small
the way
the springs coil into
staggered
floors keeps me ancient.

beskhu, the third love,
blinds me
in my second eye
but not
the third the way this
makes me
feel torn becomes a
birth in
and of itself born
wondrous
kinetic dust roams
lost in
a child's attic
plinky
plonking in the dark.

Ben Armstrong

by divinity or unfavourable mutation (a murder)

we were spearheading the attack with bottlenose dolphins
slung under our arms as makeshift bayonets when we saw
the ground rise up out of the surf, coasts pinched up out of
coral-pockets, trees sprung up out of hairline fissures.

the dolphin under my arm, which I had named Gelato,[4]
was emanating clicks and thrashing around with the wind,
a leaf bent backward and unfurled by autumnal gusts.

all of us were tears, that day I remember
drops sewn below the eye of shores.

the *Doppler Effect*: the way
                the tears   rolled out of
the Czech Republic during war-time.
songs sprung taut, minds a muddle.
G li tch e d limbs/necks craned inside shells
on a day when all of us were tears.

I exclaimed   (in mind/out loud)   aghast:
*myself, Gelato, my comrades washed up into a giant shell
that roared the way the small shells
    roared when put to an ear   or heart.*

miles off, the white crow[5] cocooned us
with a leer, as if to say
the end, the start:
all hell.

When I awoke at Ocean Terminal, a crow pecked
my sleeping sockets as if to say, 'wake up, actually

 wake up'.

dawn

shh.

eyes flutter open
                across the world one
                              eye-lid at a time.

the haze clears and light
                filters
                      in

hear   that   humming?

each filament in his bed
wriggling against the current.

Ben Armstrong

22 Ocean Terminal
a sijo

I'm standing here, at Ocean Terminal,
        wondering what happened.

Moon cut, a glass eye, light bends;
      an unusual sequin.

Like I've never seen before, light
       dies, wondering what happened.

My arm round you we see the stars
     die, the moon cut through

us as if it can see right through
      us, together, trembling as if …

I'm eating an ice cream.
    You want some.   *Us and Them* plays loud.

What I'm anticipating now
    is far too unthinkable

I am thinking, it is not fit
     for the lobe of a simpleton.

In tongues, I whisper it
     To an already dead cow, moo

I make the sound for it because
     It would have, had it been alive.
He was a bovine delight, he
   was all I had, for a long time.

Burying the cow, I notice
   you've gone

and all I've left is dirt.

III – Ouroboros

III – Ouroboros

[bandstand blues]

boot juice.
there's soot in the air
tonight I can't stand you.
I've got the blues.
– aching, the exoskeletal bandstand
sways in the   faux breeze,
pretends to
dance in the   real wind
as we, within it,
decide to give way.

it's real easy –
nodding percussion boy/
daydream french horn girl/   *are ill suited:*
like it/lump it.
and guess who's the bad guy?
me with grey guillotine coat on
me with ashtray mouth
me with the "unsuitable
for dates" snare drum
– "unflattering", even –
which I had chosen
especially
to woo
you
in
this
bandstand:
the exoskeletal bastard.

Ben Armstrong

poseidon

poseidon roars at the power outage
at the power station on windsurf jetty
                      sailor jerry engineered for forty years.

coral reef pours its damn heart out
brushing past dislodged mussels it's
                      memorised at thirty knots.

trident tickles the surf first,then bludgeons.
The red sea is born
                      of a virgin blade, the first casualty.

the kingfisher population nearly extinct,
poseidon sits
casually toques his pipe,
eyes flecked flames.

pygmy offering

boy, ligan, light up! & be my virgil
                                    handed
                                                  down
through flotsam prisons
                  the way
        the wind
would want.

knead barked gusts into blizzards
    on the hunt for the bandied-down denizens

furnishing the coffee-houses of sturgeons
                                the way
                                        the tide
would want.
all
things
smash against poseidon's
                axe-handled fist,

surf creases you//
//o ri g am i, bream-cry
fresh in the ears, coasts' hands thumb
down.

the whale king extends a flipper,
walk with him   [...?]

Ben Armstrong

homer's ring

and it is with large fins that we hug the world
and with great joy that we are fit to praise our god[6]
and the chorus of calves burst into rapture
at the sound of this last line, as if Martin Luther King
were looking down on them, imbuing the scene with a
somehow weightier stroke; each phrase brushed onto
each calf as if they were meant to feel this way.

and[7] it was around then that
a great hunger rose up inside me
to learn the Odyssean ways of the whales,
– each now pulsing ultraviolet
               brambled with lightning -
as they melted from song to song;
an equator of violaceae
halo'd round a heart.

it would not be long before I wished fins from out my shoulders
gained the taste for krill
and prayed for a metamorphosis[8] that made spout my fontanelle.

a breath

(a whale call on the wind)
passes through   just-so
– a yawn at breakfast.
making demands of baristas
one
long
question.

[the whale song eminates from the cave]

& it was precisely three o clock
of last week the third of   a month that
escapes me, the day of which   eludes me that
the coffee house's rich oak walls
made me its embryo
               its bean.

(krill krill krill krill krill krill krill krill krill)

everything the whales say is in parentheses
precisely as w i   d   e
                     as they need to be
& with no line breaks no pause for breath
– a hum to last a lifetime.

entering the cave I see
the whales bunched
together in antique clusters,
                as if in
saccharine seas, on
waveless summer days.

atlas

the atlas threw off the shawl of the antarctic.
the atlantic flipped up oil tankers, a renegade tablecloth.
the myth of moby dick leveraged all its might into one movement.
the ocean strangled its own hemlock.

cale made mosaics of blank spaces,
punctured beds with swoons the dolphins
chattered tunes to wake the urchins, moon
cracked tide in two.

our ahab died in shallow waters.
molluscs shelled him up and carried
corpse on corpse up to the silt bank.
a cracked fishtank bled a castle.

the atlas threw off the skin it had been sewn
                 – leveraged its whole weight –

to strangle the ocean.

The Blue Ringed Octopus

The Blue Ringed Octopus dispenses its ink cartridge,
screaming *octopodes!* from dark recesses.

Irritable/glows iridescent blue,
undresses you and
pops out from an alcove/
gives you the wretched prod.

Wintertime but no snow in the oceans
only colder.
Sea-life given the cold-shoulder the
               life   ender

but warmth of magma keeps Octopus ticking over.
Always coiled and
shacked up in some
shabby hole

but a hole that is a home, nonetheless:
decorated with cadavers/pillowed seaweed,
bloody capes/
crowns of skulls of all our
failed baliffs
left delicate/stagnating
to taste.

old bar

in the old bar, giants creak on their seats;
beard's crumb keepsakes: sweet, roasted.
toasting to good health and with
lurid smiles, they try to decode it all,
this din, a dram.

                        hands span whole equators
entire   oceans   old
equations, tired prose.
they're half
    -cut digressives with paper cuts from
paperbacks and chestnuts as their
       >>>   >> rafts.

in the old bar, they're part of the furniture,
wild or something child-
like lurching though each a moon in mass.

we're chairs and rickety, remember,
[many don't]
& should we
sink —
      we don't discourage drinking
in our memory.

Coca Cola Focus Group

[men on wheeley chairs are spinning furiously around at Coca Cola HQ][9]

This cannot be happening
one of them is saying with punctuation ?!
/another crossing himself for an imagined audience.

All the computer screens are blue, have given up, scowling.
Ambient background hum now bee growl.

Richardson punches in some integers
/Johnson rallies the troops around the confectionary machine,
shovels up the suicides with a corporate smile.

[dolly zoom: small orange can in containment cube. The Cause of All This]

We should have known, Hecker!
Charleston says, doing the Charleston.

There's talk of a prophecy.
Men battle
for weeks
over the graph paper
which iterates
in one way or another
that they're all
doomed.

endless

I eschew rhyming words
for *midsts, sowthed, bulb.*
I'm obliged/
                out of my depth, to speak
on such
a thing
as rhyme;
        that wolf's howl trapped in Ginsberg's
throat he sculpts from out his vulns.

kirsch kirsch kirsch k i r s c h.
We film language drunk from through the television.
the way glass holds the sound *fugue*
or is it *jougs*
                [in any case]
they cadence
beautifully.

lonely genus

With you, it's terraforming comfort zones.
Without me, sea monkey habitat goes
smash; we spend all our time repairing homes.
You, inside, watching all the concrete prose
wobble like loose eyes. Wave, insomniac –
your fixed gaze crisscrossed, upturned. The sad shoal
follows me. I'm building them a brand new home,
(the last) made crumb in a flash by a black hole.

My friends, the fish, repay me with treasure
which I invest in a pensioners trust
for old fish, to keep them old but clever.
Me inside, spent, watching the whole sea rust.
I learn to live without necessity,
This flood made drought by sand,
                    sans you, sans me.

Ben Armstrong

Berwick's Jaw

sometimes I entertain the belief that
the whale jaw is on the hill because
a whale died there back when everything
was waves, or on other days that a whale
clambered up onto that very hill out
of curiosity and fell prey to
a vicious bout of asphyxia.

one day I saw the jaw dislocate the
sun from its slumber, so I named it Ray
after the sun's rays which it
ate whole.

~

we're always
climbing up
on top of
hills finding
we're just teeth.

colossal
for d.t.

& the ground
opens up
midway through
the *Lord of the Rings* soundtrack.

blast we say
as we sail away
into silence.

& the mountain sighs
[a huge sigh of]
relief when the biters arrive,
clearing away the clutter of
bipedal life.

& thank goodness we're
                            up here
watching waves crack
gaping sky claps
[round of applause]
& we're amused.

the truth is
I never want to leave this place
a place where
[without warning]
a downpour can rain us all away
just as far as it wants.

& when the rain
has had its fill,
o'erbrimming tidal breath
takes the place which we called
home –
returns it, just a hill.

& when we think we're far enough
we're even further still.

Ben Armstrong

soulcollector I

up
to the gills in krill
I spend a long time
grazing on the souls
I've come across in skulls.

[one had raged as Achilles raged,
murderous,
one fawning for the sea found
a cove]

the girl I love best
– the mermaid's skull
I keep in my capes
        for safe
  keeping
          – lonely and cut through with quay-scars,
eye-sockets impressions of pearls.

[the tears
came years
before the rot trickled in/
the steely grey soul of a
half and
    half.   The soul snapped
a
nut
in
a
cracker]

bulbous brain
DNA rearranged.
I am all of
  you   arrest me with your stare.

Perennial: Notes from a Weatherproof Journal

?

play me at 33 first
let your fingers run across
my grooves, stab me into singing
my etched meaning, let the needle

run its course and leave me.

love lost across oceans

Ben Armstrong

?...

the whip
cracked the
jetty years ago and
made the
distance
between the lighthouses
concrete.
surf draws
the imaginary
                line   ~~~

the pier
for k.b.

the gargantuan pier swallowed you as a bullet
in a fresh wound on a day where kites were swallowed
by the skies' typhoon -

it's true
I followed myself home behind
a cloud of powder,
watched you launched out of a
makeshift pipeorgan,
felt you turn and section me
with lighthouse fire.

art is a liar said the parrot
who had learnt words
arbitrarily and it got me thinking about art and if
the meaning of the piece was a meaning, or even
meant.

the sea cucumbers could care less as we zero'd the steel,
red wine surreally green and sipped down in integers
until our bodies learned unorthodox beats and our
bones broke, two twigs in a breeze.

         a
        boat
        ↓

passed   through the
green   and red beacons
laid   out and
longing   to be together

the ship a conduit for love lost across oceans
seemed still on a night
where the moon was bloated and bright;
a balloon we'd let go
from a pier
we'd built long before.

Notes

1. a land mass stuck in soup so longing for home that the croutons have sunken.

2. a bibliotheque of decrepit bones ... spines

3. grey-green world of spores//the putrefied mortar//both bricks dear life//bricks deep depth

4. On account of his squishiness, which, thankfully didn't extend to his temperament; he was, after all, a fine bayonet.

5. Which was white either by divinity or an unfavourable mutation.

6. Presumably krill, or the monarch of the krill – that much I hadn't yet discovered.

7. it was around then that ceremonial buckets of krill were passed around the circle

8. Although living absolutely as a whale during the course of the project would considerably speed up the process of discovery, I would, perhaps, miss opposable thumbs were I a whale – so consider this image a '"metaphor" morphosis' of sorts.

9. Did you know: Irn Bru is *still* the biggest selling soft drink brand in Scotland, despite gratuitous (and unsuccessful) marketing campaigns by rival brand, and recognised carbonated beverage world leader, Coca Cola Co.